W9-DFD-981

Backyard Animals
Bison

Tatiana Tomljanovic

www.av2books.com

AV² by Weigl brings you media enhanced books that support active learning.

AV² provides enriched content that supplements and complements this book. Weigl's AV² books strive to create inspired learning and engage young minds for a total learning experience.

Go to **www.av2books.com**, and enter this book's unique code. You will have access to video, audio, web links, quizzes, a slide show, and activities.

BOOK CODE

N574366

Audio
Listen to sections of the book read aloud.

Video
Watch informative video clips.

Web Link
Find research sites and play interactive games.

Try This!
Complete activities and hands-on experiments.

Due to the dynamic nature of the Internet, some of the URLs and activities provided as part of AV² by Weigl may have changed or ceased to exist. AV² by Weigl accepts no responsibility for any such changes. All media enhanced books are regularly monitored to update addresses and sites in a timely manner. Contact AV² by Weigl at 1-866-649-3445 or av2books@weigl.com with any questions, comments, or feedback.

Published by AV² by Weigl
350 5th Avenue, 59th Floor
NewYork, NY 10118
Website: www.av2books.com   www.weigl.com

Library of Congress Cataloging-in-Publication Data

Tomljanovic, Tatiana.
 Bison / Tatiana Tomljanovic.
    p. cm. -- (Backyard animals)
 Includes index.
 ISBN 978-1-60596-955-8 (hardcover : alk. paper) -- ISBN 978-1-60596-956-5 (softcover : alk. paper) --
 ISBN 978-1-60596-957-2 (e-book)
 1. American bison--Juvenile literature. I. Title.
 QL737.U53T66 2010
 599.64'3--dc22
                              2009050309

Printed in the United States of America in North Mankato, Minnesota
1 2 3 4 5 6 7 8 9 0 14 13 12 11 10

042010

WEP264000

Editor Heather C. Hudak   **Design** Terry Paulhus

Every reasonable effort has been made to trace ownership and to obtain permission to reprint copyright material. The publishers would be pleased to have any errors or omissions brought to their attention so that they may be corrected in subsequent printings.

Photo Credits
Weigl acknowledges Getty Images as its primary photo supplier for this title.

Contents

Meet the Bison

American bison are the largest land **mammals** in North America. They are about 5 to 6 feet (1.5 to 1.8 meters) tall at the shoulder and weigh as much as a car. Bison have thick, shaggy fur that is dark brown or black in color. They have a hump at the shoulders and a short tail with a tassel. Males have a beard on their chin.

Bison live mostly on the open plains or prairies of North America. Here, there is little to protect them from poor weather. Bison sometimes huddle together to keep each other warm.

Bison live in small groups called bands. Sometimes, bands join together to form a large herd. In nature, herds travel from place to place to find food and avoid **predators**.

When the first Europeans came to North America, they thought bison looked like Asian and African animals called buffalo. They called bison "buffalo" after these animals.

Bison are sometimes called buffalo.

All about Bison

There are two types of American bison. Plains bison can be found on the **Great Plains**, from southern Canada to Mexico. Wood bison are found in forests in Alaska and northwestern Canada.

At one time, there were more plains bison than any other grazing animal on the North American plains. Today, there about 500,000 bison in North America. Most of these are raised on ranches. Less than 30,000 are part of herds in parks and refuges.

Bison sometimes lock horns and push at each other. They do this to fight for rank within a group.

Bison Relatives

Wisent

- Weighs between 660 and 2,000 pounds (299 and 907 kilograms)
- Can be 10 feet (3 m) long and 6 to 7 feet (1.8 to 2.1 m) tall

Wood Bison

- Males can weigh up to 2,000 pounds (907 kg)

Yak

- Males weigh 2,200 pounds (998 kg) and are 6.6 to 7.2 feet (2 to 2.2 m) tall
- Females weigh a third of an average male

Water Buffalo

- Weigh up to 2,600 pounds (1,179 kg)
- Grow to be 8 to 9 feet (2.4 to 2.7 m) long and 6.6 feet (2 m) tall

African Buffalo

- Weigh up to 1,500 pounds (680 kg)
- Grow to be 4.4 to 5.6 feet (1.3 to 1.7 m) tall and 7 to 11 feet (2.1 to 3.4 m) long

Cattle

- Males weigh between 1,000 and 4,000 pounds (454 and 1,814 kg)
- Females weigh 1,000 to 1,400 pounds (454 to 635 kg)

Bison History

Bison are an important symbol of life in the western United States. For hundreds of years, American Indians hunted bison for food, shelter, and tools.

In the 19th century, there were more than 50 million bison. By the early 20th century, European settlers began hunting bison for food and for fun. Over time, the bison had been hunted almost to **extinction**. Many American Indians were forced to find new ways to live since so few bison remained.

By the late 1800s, settlers realized they needed to protect the bison to keep it from becoming extinct. Laws were passed to stop bison hunting. The remaining bison were given safe places to live, such as parks and refuges.

Many people thought wood bison no longer lived any place on Earth. A herd of 200 was found in Alberta, Canada, in 1957.

Early American Indians hunted bison with bows and arrows or spears.

Bison Shelter

Many animals build shelters, such as dens or nests. Others live in caves or trees. Bison do not need a special place to live. They live on the open land of the prairies. Bison herds live within a home range. Home ranges can cover 66 to 480 square miles (171 to 1,243 square kilometers).

On the flat ground of the prairies, there are few places to hide from predators. Bison keep safe by staying with their herd. Few animals are large enough to attack a single bison. Grizzly bears, cougars, and wolves may sometimes attack young or weak bison. Predators must separate their prey from the herd.

Most bison herds include a mix of females, babies, and a few males. The remaining bulls form their own groups.

In nature, bison herds are only found in a few parks and refuges.

Bison Features

Bison have special body parts that allow them to survive on the prairies. Their thick fur protects them from the harsh weather on open grasslands. Each year, bison shed their lighter summer coat and grow a thick new one for the winter. The winter coat is well **insulated**. Snow can land on a bison's coat without being melted by its body heat. This is just one of the bison's many **adaptations**.

TAIL

A bison's tail is good for swatting away insects. Sometimes, male bison raise their tails straight up. This is a way to show **dominance**. A male with an upright tail may attack another male. Female bison raise their tails to warn the herd of danger.

LEGS

Despite their large size, bison can run very fast and for a long time. They lift their legs as little as possible when they run. This uses small amounts of energy. Their strong leg muscles also help keep bison moving quickly.

HUMP

The large hump on a bison's back is made of bone and muscle. It supports the bison's large head. Buffalo do not have this hump.

HORNS

Both males and female bison have sharp horns. They use their horns to protect themselves from predators. Males also use their horns to fight each other during mating season. Some males use their horns often. They have ring-shaped markings from wear.

EYES AND NOSE

Bison have a very poor sense of sight. They make up for this with an excellent sense of smell and good hearing. In fact, bison can detect scents up to 1.9 miles (3 km) away.

BEARD

Bison have a thick beard. Both females and males have beards. Buffalo, the cousins of bison, do not have beards.

What Do Bison Eat?

Bison are herbivores. This means that they only eat plants, such as grass and shrubs. Bison eat up to five times each day. In winter, plants are often covered by snow. Bison use their muzzle and hoofs to clear away the snow and find food.

Like cattle, bison can eat plants that are too rough or hard for most other animals. This is because they have a special stomach. Bison chew and swallow their food. This food is broken down in the first stomach. After a while, this food is **regurgitated** and chewed again. The regurgitated food is called cud. After chewing the cud to break it down more, the bison swallows. The cud moves to the second stomach, where it is broken down more. This process helps bison get more **nutrients** from their food.

Some plants contain a mineral that is rough and wears down teeth. For this reason, older bison will have shorter teeth than younger ones.

Bison droppings help grass grow in places where these animals graze. Bison return to graze at these places when the grass has regrown.

Bison Life Cycle

Adult male bison are called bulls. Bulls compete with each other during mating season. This takes place between July and September. Sometimes, bulls are injured during the fights. Only the strongest bulls get to mate. After the bison mate, the herd splits into smaller bands.

Birth

Baby bison are called calves. Calves are reddish-brown in color and weigh between 20 and 70 pounds (9 and 32 kg). They are born without humps or horns. Calves' legs are as long as their parents' legs, and they are able to run within a few hours of birth. This helps calves escape if a predator attacks.

One Day to One Year

Cows are protective of their calves. Calves stay close to their mother for the first week. After a few weeks, calves may leave their mothers to play with other calves. An older cow watches the calves while they play. The cow may not have a calf of her own. Calves drink their mother's milk until they are six to eight months old. They grow quickly and can weigh between 400 and 600 pounds (181 and 272 kg) after one year.

Female bison are called cows. They give birth to baby bison about nine months after mating, between April and June. A cow usually moves away from the herd while giving birth. Cows give birth to one baby at a time. The cow and her baby will stay away from the herd for a few days.

Adult

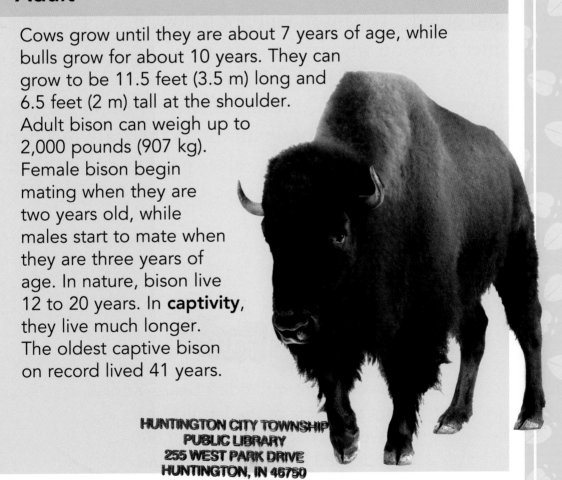

Cows grow until they are about 7 years of age, while bulls grow for about 10 years. They can grow to be 11.5 feet (3.5 m) long and 6.5 feet (2 m) tall at the shoulder. Adult bison can weigh up to 2,000 pounds (907 kg). Female bison begin mating when they are two years old, while males start to mate when they are three years of age. In nature, bison live 12 to 20 years. In **captivity**, they live much longer. The oldest captive bison on record lived 41 years.

Encountering Bison

A herd of bison may seem calm, but it can be easily frightened. If they sense danger, bison prefer to run than to fight. They will scatter about in many directions. This is called a stampede. Stampeding bison can harm people who are in their path.

People should always keep their distance from a bison. If a bison is nearby, it is best to move away very slowly and quietly. The bison will not follow. Bison may chase after a person who tries to run away.

Bison need a certain amount of space around them to feel safe. The more dominant males there are in a herd, the more space they need. Calves need less space than adult bison.

Bison can fight off kodiak bears. Kodiak bears are some of the largest bears in the world. They weigh up to 1,500 pounds (680 kilograms) and stand 10 feet (3 meters) tall.

Bison can run as fast as
40 miles (64 km) per hour.

Myths and Legends

American Indians needed the bison to survive. They respected the animal because it provided them with food and shelter. They used every part of the animal. Hides were used to make clothing and shelter. Hoofs were used to make glue, while the bones were made into tools and weapons.

The Blackfoot Indians tell a story about how Creator Sun made the bison. The story says that Creator Sun took some of the mud that he used to make the first human, and molded an animal with four legs, a head, and a body. He held the animal to his mouth and blew hard into its nose. The animal came to life and began to breathe. Its meat was given to the first humans. It was a gift from Creator Sun. This animal became known as the bison.

The state flag of Wyoming was decided in a contest in 1916, and chosen in 1917. The flag shows a bison with the state seal on its body.

Race for Chief

The Cheyenne Indians tell a story of a race between bison and humans.

Bison was the largest of all animals and wanted to be chief. Humans also wanted to rule over all of the animals. They decided to hold a race to see who should be in charge. The humans thought the race would not be fair because they had only two legs, while bison had four. They chose the Bird People to race in their place.

At first, Hummingbird was leading the race, but its wings were too small to keep pace. Meadowlark and Hawk tried to outrun Bison, but their wings became tired. Bison was nearing the finish line when Magpie flew past him. The two pushed hard to reach the finish first. The race was very close. As Bison ran, he kicked up so much dust the other animals could not see who crossed the line first. When the dust settled, they could see that Magpie had won. The humans would now rule Earth.

Frequently Asked Questions

Why do bison have a hump on their back?

Answer: Bison live where there is deep snow in the winter. In order to reach the grasses that they eat, they push snow away with their heads. The large hump on their backs is made up of strong muscles that help them move snow.

Why do bison roll around in the dirt?

Answer: Rolling around in the dirt is known as wallowing. Bison create wallows by scraping a bare spot in the ground with their hoofs. They roll around in the wallow so that dirt is ground into their coats. The dirt protects them from bug bites and the cold when it rains.

What sounds do bison make?

Answer: Unlike cattle, bison do not moo or bawl. They make grunting or roaring sounds.

Words to Know

adaptations: features that help an animal live in certain conditions

captivity: kept in a confined space

dominance: stronger or more fit than another animal in the group

extinction: a state of no longer living any place on Earth

Great Plains: a huge prairie area east of the Rocky Mountains that reaches from Texas to the Mackenzie River in Canada

insulated: protected from cold or hot weather

mammals: warm-blooded animals that have fur, give birth to live young, and make milk for their babies

nutrients: substances that provide food for healthy growth

predators: animals that hunt other animals for food

regurgitated: food that is thrown up after eating

Index

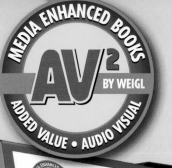

Log on to www.av2books.com

AV² by Weigl brings you media enhanced books that support active learning. Go to **www.av2books.com**, and enter the special code inside the front cover of this book. You will gain access to enriched and enhanced content that supplements and complements this book. Content includes video, audio, web links, quizzes, a slide show, and activities.

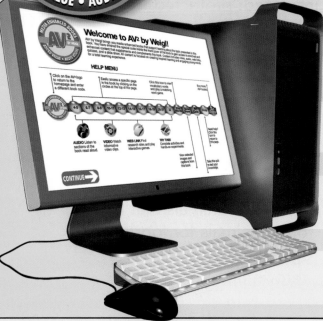

Audio
Listen to sections of the book read aloud.

Video
Watch informative video clips.

Web Link
Find research sites and play interactive games.

Try This!
Complete activities and hands-on experiments.

WHAT'S ONLINE?

Try This!
Complete activities and hands-on experiments.

Pages 6-7 identify bison relatives.

Pages 12-13 List six important features of the bison.

Pages 16-17 Compare the similarities and differences between a bison calf and an adult bison.

Page 22 Test your bison knowledge.

Web Link
Find research sites and play interactive games.

Pages 6-7 Learn about wood bison and plains bison.

Pages 8-9 Find more about the history of bison in North America.

Pages 10-11 Play an interactive bison game.

Pages 18-19 Find out fascinating facts about bison.

Pages 20-21 Read more stories about bison.

Video
Watch informative video clips.

Pages 4-5 Watch a video about American bison.

Pages 10-11 See how bison live in nature.

Pages 14-15 Watch a bison eating.

EXTRA FEATURES

Audio
Hear introductory audio at the top of every page

Key Words
Study vocabulary, and play a matching word game.

Slide Show
View images and captions, and try a writing activity.

AV² Quiz
Take this quiz to test your knowledge